Addison-Wesley
Science

Authors

Charles Barman, Ed.D.
Associate Professor of Science Education
Indiana University, Indianapolis

Michael DiSpezio, M.A.
Science Department Chairman
Cape Cod Academy, Massachusetts

Vallie Guthrie, Ph.D.
Director, Greensboro Area Math
and Science Education Center
North Carolina Agricultural and Technical
State University

Michael B. Leyden, Ed.D.
Professor of Education
Eastern Illinois University

Sheryl Mercier, M.A.
Elementary Science Specialist
Fresno Unified School District,
California

Karen Ostlund, Ph.D.
Associate Professor of Education
Southwest Texas State University

Reading Consultant

Bonnie Armbruster, Ph.D.
Associate Professor
Center for the Study of Reading and
Department of Elementary and Early
Childhood Education
University of Illinois

 Addison-Wesley Publishing Company

Menlo Park, California • Reading, Massachusetts • New York
Don Mills, Ontario • Wokingham, England • Amsterdam • Bonn
Sydney • Singapore • Tokyo • Madrid • Bogotá • Santiago • San Juan

Content Consultants

Thomas H. Callen II, Ph.D.
Program Resource Manager
Albert Einstein Planetarium
National Air and Space Museum
Smithsonian Institution

Jym Ganahl
Chief Meteorologist
WCMH-TV, Columbus, Ohio

Edwin Harper, Ph.D.
Associate Professor of Biochemistry
Indiana University School of Medicine

Robert W. Hinds, Ph.D.
Professor of Geology
Slippery Rock University, Pennsylvania

Chelcie Liu, Ph.D.
Physics Instructor
City College of San Francisco

Luis A. Martinez-Perez, Ph.D.
Associate Professor of Science Education
Florida International University

Linda Medleau, D.V.M., M.S.
Assistant Professor
Department of Small Animal Medicine
University of Georgia

Larry K. Pickering, M.D.
Professor of Pediatrics and Director of
Pediatric Infectious Diseases
University of Texas Medical School at Houston

Linda Sanford
Curator of Youth Education
Morton Arboretum, Lisle, Illinois

Lydia Young, Ph.D.
Senior Engineer
Perkin-Elmer Electron Beam Technology
Hayward, California

Critical Thinking Consultant
Robert Swartz, Ph.D.
Director of Critical and Creative Thinking Program
University of Massachusetts, Boston

Safety Consultant
Jay A. Young, Ph.D.
Chemical Consultant
Silver Spring, Maryland

Testing Consultant
David P. Butts, Ph.D.
Aderhold Distinguished Professor
College of Education
University of Georgia

Cover Photos: Raccoons
Front cover: Gary Milburn/Tom Stack & Associates
Back cover: Joe McDonald/Tom Stack & Associates

ISBN 0-201-25410-7

EFGHIJKL-VH- 9210

Getting to Know
Addison-Wesley Science

This book was made to help you
learn science.
It has things for you to read about
and to think about.
It has things for you to do.
You will learn by reading.
You will learn by thinking.
You will learn by doing things, too.

Contents

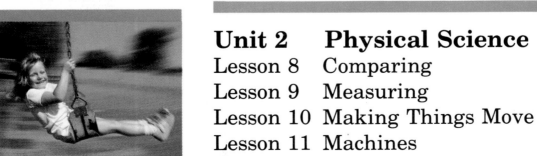

What Is Science?

Science is learning about the world
around you.
It is looking at things.
It is listening to things.
Science is using all of your senses.

Scientists ask many questions.
They try to find the answers.
They write down what they see
and hear.
Scientists study what they write down.
This helps them learn about the world.

Reading About Science

You can learn science by reading.
You can read all the words carefully.
You can learn what the words
in **dark type** mean.
They are important science words.
You can read the questions carefully.
And you can look closely at the pictures.

Thinking About Science

You can learn science by thinking
about what you read and do.
You can ask lots of questions.
Then you can try to find the answers
to your questions.

Doing Science Activities

You can learn science by doing
activities.
Read the directions and look
at the pictures.
Try to guess what will happen.
Watch and listen.
Think about what happens.
Try to explain what you see and hear.

Safety in Science

Scientists are careful when they work.
You need to be careful, too.

Read all the directions before you
begin an activity.
Do each step in order.
Never smell or taste things
unless your teacher says it is safe.
Be extra careful when you see ◇.
Clean up when you are done.

Unit One
Life Science

Life science is about living things.
It is about animals and plants.
It is learning how animals eat,
move, and keep safe.
It is learning what plants need
to live.

Lesson 1
How Animals Move

Getting Started

Moving Like an Animal

1. Use animal pictures.

2. Choose one picture. Do not let anyone see it.

3. Show others how your animal moves. Do not make any animal sounds.

4. Let the others guess your animal.

Some **animals** walk, run, or jump.
They use legs.

Other animals fly.
They use wings.

Some animals swim.
They use fins or flippers.

Other animals crawl.
They do not have legs.
They do not have wings or fins.

Some animals **move** very fast.

Other animals move slowly.

Animals move to get food.
They move to get away from danger.
They move to feed their babies.

Look at the pictures.
Why does each animal move?

Finding Out

Use these things:
earthworm
box lid
damp paper towel
hand lens
pencil

Find out how an earthworm moves.

1. Put the damp paper towel in the box lid.

2. ◇ **Handle with care!** Put the worm on top of the paper towel.

3. Use the hand lens.
   Look at the worm.
   Watch it move.

4. Use the eraser end of a pencil.
   Carefully touch the worm.
   Watch it move.

How did the earthworm move?

Lesson 1 Checkup

1. How does the animal move?
   Match the words with the pictures.

crawl   swim   walk   fly

2. Tell why each animal is moving.

3. Think! Tell how each animal moved.

 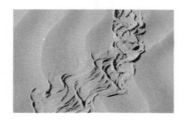

Lesson 2
How Animals Eat

Getting Started

Learning How You Eat

1. Use a juice bar, pencil, paper plate, and paper.

2. Lick the juice bar. Suck on the juice bar.

3. Bite off a piece of the juice bar. Chew it.

4. Draw what you used to lick the juice bar. Draw what you used to suck on it. Draw what you used to bite the juice bar.

Animals must eat to live.
Some animals are **plant eaters**.
Some animals are **meat eaters**.
Some animals eat plants and animals.
What do you eat?

Animals eat in many ways.

A snake swallows its food whole.

A frog gets food with its tongue.
The tongue is very long.
Bugs stick to it.

Many animals have teeth.

Meat eaters have sharp teeth.

Plant eaters have flat teeth.

Birds do not have teeth.
They get food with their beaks.

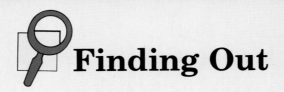

Finding Out

Use these things:
jar with lid
caterpillar
twigs
leaves
hand lens

Find out how a caterpillar eats.

1. Find a caterpillar.
Place it in a jar.

2. Put some twigs in the jar.

3. Put some leaves in the jar.
Use two kinds of leaves.
Add fresh leaves every day.

4. Watch the caterpillar eat.

How did the caterpillar eat?

What leaves did it eat?

Lesson 2 Checkup

1. Match the words with the pictures.

teeth   beak   tongue

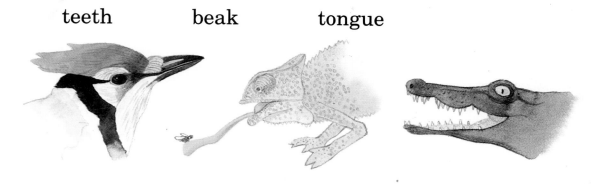

2. Tell which animals are plant eaters.

3. Think! Tell how these animals are alike.

Lesson 3
Animal Body Coverings

Getting Started

Looking at Animal Body Coverings

1. Use animal body coverings, a hand lens, a dropper, and water.

2. Close your eyes. Feel the animal coverings.

3. Use the hand lens. Look closely at the coverings.

4. Put a little water on the coverings. Feel under them.

All animals have **body coverings**.
Some animals have feathers.
Some animals have fur.

Some animals have scales.
Others have a shell.

What body coverings do these animals have?

Body coverings can keep animals warm and dry.

Body coverings can keep animals safe.

Body coverings are different colors.
Colors can keep animals safe.
Can you find the animals?

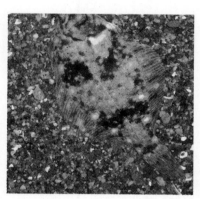

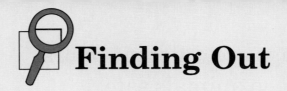

Finding Out

Use these things:
animal coverings
blindfold

Find out how body coverings can help animals hide.

1. Work with a partner.
   Choose a pair of animal coverings.

2. Have your partner put on
   a blindfold.

3. Put the coverings in two places.
   Put them where they can be seen.
   Make one hard to find.
   Make the other one easy to find.

4. Let your partner take off
   the blindfold.
   Ask your partner to find
   the coverings.

Which covering was found first?

What made it easier to find?

36

Lesson 3 Checkup

1. Name the body covering in each picture.
Name two animals for each covering.

2. Tell what keeps the animal safe.

3. Think! Tell which one does not
belong. Tell why.

Lesson 4
People Use Animals

Getting Started

Finding Things That Come from Animals

1. Use animal stickers.

2. Look at the things you are wearing. Look around the room. Find things that come from animals.

3. Choose an animal sticker. Put it on something that comes from that animal.

People use animals in many ways.

People use animals for food.

We get honey from bees.
We get eggs from hens.

We use many animals for meat.

We get milk from cows.

Milk can be used to make other foods.
Can you name some?

People use feathers from geese
to stuff things.

People use wool from sheep
to make cloth.

People use animals to do work.

People enjoy animals, too.

 # Finding Out

Use these things:
jar with lid
cream
cracker
plastic knife

Find out how butter is made.

1. Wash your hands.

2. Pour a little cream in the jar.

3. Close the lid.

4. Shake the jar very hard.

5. Look inside.
   Shake some more.
   Shake until the cream changes.

6. Put the butter on the cracker
   and eat.

**What made the cream turn
into butter?**

**What animal is needed to make
butter?**

44

Lesson 4 Checkup

1. Match the pictures.
Find a use for each animal.

2. Think! Tell how you could use
this animal.
Name as many ways as you can.

Lesson 5
Plants

Getting Started

Looking at a Plant

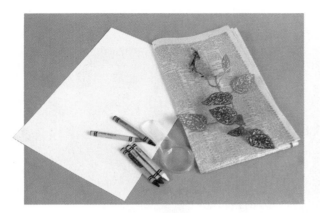

1. Use newspapers,
a plant, a hand lens,
paper, and crayons.

2. Pick up the plant.
Look carefully at it.
Look for different parts.

3. Use the hand lens.
Look at all parts
of the plant.

4. Draw a picture
of the plant.

Look at all the **plants**.
They have different sizes, shapes,
and colors.

Plants are alike in two ways.
They stay in one place.
And they make their own food.

Plants use air, water, and light
to make food.

Plants have three main parts.
Find the parts in the picture.

Some plants have one big **root**.
Other plants have roots
with many parts.

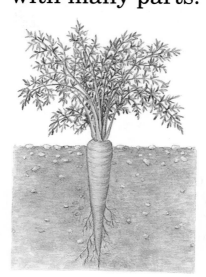
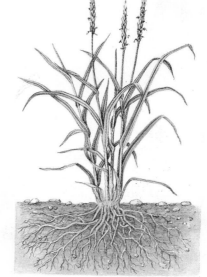

Some plants have hard **stems**.
Other plants have soft stems.

Some stems are tall.
Other stems are short.
Some stems grow along the ground.

Plant **leaves** can be many sizes
and shapes.
They can be big or small.
They can be smooth or jagged.
They can even look like big needles.

Plants may have other parts, too.

Many plants have **flowers**, **fruits**, and **seeds**.

Some plants have **cones**.
The cones have seeds in them.

53

Finding Out

Use these things:
carrot root top
dish

Find out how plant parts grow.

1. Place the top of a carrot root
in a dish.
Put the cut side down.

2. Cover most of the root
with water.

3. Put fresh water in the dish
each day.
Do not let the carrot get dry.

4. What do you think will grow
out of the top of the carrot?
What do you think will grow
out of the bottom of the carrot?

5. Wait and watch.

**What plant parts grew
from the carrot root? Where?**

Lesson 5 Checkup

1. Match the word with each picture.

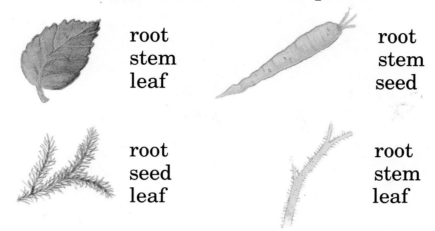

root
stem
leaf

root
stem
seed

root
seed
leaf

root
stem
leaf

2. Match the word with each picture.

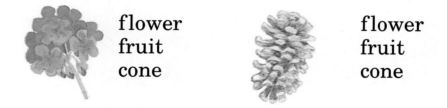

flower
fruit
cone

flower
fruit
cone

3. Think! Name two main ways that plants are different from animals.

Lesson 6
People Use Plants

Getting Started

Finding Things That Come from Plants

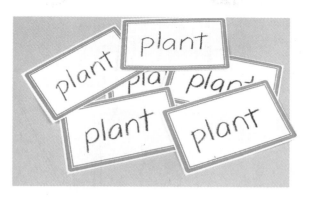

1. Use plant stickers.

2. Look at the things you are wearing. Look around the room. Find things that come from plants.

3. Put the plant stickers on the things that come from plants.

57

People use plants for food.
Some roots and stems are good to eat.
So are some kinds of leaves.
We even eat some plant flowers.
What plant parts are in the pictures?

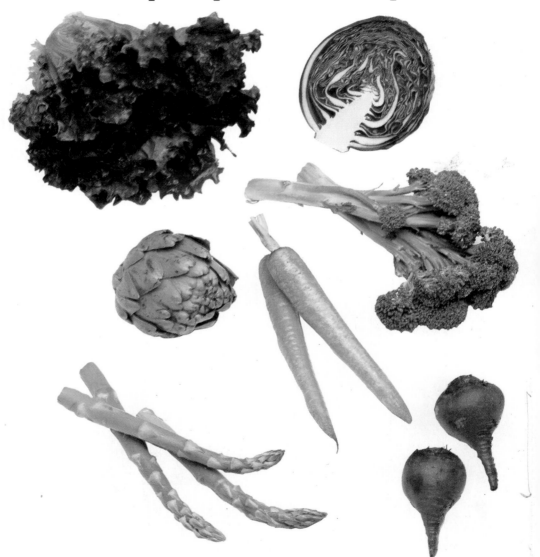

People eat many fruits and seeds.

The wheat plant has seeds.
We grind the seeds to make flour.
We use flour to make other foods.

People make things from plants.

We use wood from trees to make many different things.

We make cloth from cotton plants.
We make baskets from bamboo.

We enjoy plants, too.

Finding Out

Use these things:
pieces of beet
cup
hot water
cloth

Find out how cloth can be dyed.

1. Put three large pieces of beet in a cup.

2. ◇ **Hot!** Pour in some hot water. Wait awhile.

3. Fold a cloth a few times.

4. Put a corner in the bowl. Wait awhile. Put another corner in. Wait again.

5. Take the cloth out. Let it dry.

6. Open up the cloth.

What made the color in the cloth?

Lesson 6 Checkup

1. What part of the plant is each food?

2. Which things are made from plants?

3. Think! Tell how you could use this apple tree.
Name as many ways as you can.

Lesson 7
Animal and Plant Care

Getting Started

Making an Animal Home

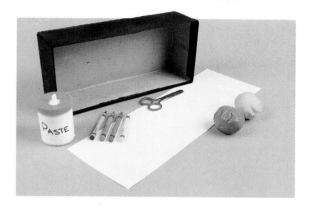

1. Use clay, crayons, paste, paper, scissors, and a box.

2. Think of any animal. Make the animal with the clay.

3. Draw the place where the animal lives. Draw what it eats and drinks.

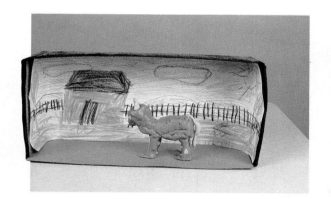

4. Paste the picture inside the box. Put your animal in its home.

Animals need food, water, and air.
They also need a safe place to live.

Wild animals find their own food,
water, and places to live.
They take care of themselves.

Sometimes we can help wild animals.

People take care of farm animals.
People take care of pets, too.
How can we take care of
farm animals?
How can we take care of pets?

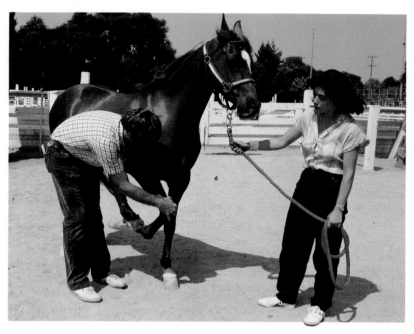

Plants need water, light, and air.
They also need the right **temperature**.
Most plants need soil, too.

Wild plants take care of themselves.

Sometimes we can help wild plants.

People take care of plants on farms.
People take care of house plants.

 **Finding Out**

Use these things:
2 plants
crayons
drawing paper

Find out if plants need water to live.

1. Put the plants in a place that has light.
Label one plant *water*.
Label one plant *no water*.

2. Water one plant the way your teacher tells you.
Do not water the other plant.

3. Look at the plants each day.
Watch them for two weeks.

4. Draw a picture of each plant on the first day.
Draw a picture of each plant after three, five, and ten days.

What happened to each plant?

Do plants need water to live?

Lesson 7 Checkup

1. Find the things that pets and farm animals need.

2. Find the things that farm plants and house plants need.

3. How can you help wild animals and plants?

4. **Think!** Choose two different pets. Tell how their needs are different. Tell how to take care of each animal.

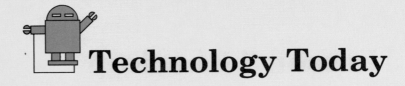 # Technology Today

From Trees to Paper

Most paper is made from wood.
It is made at a **paper mill**.

Trees are cut down in the forest.
The logs are brought to the mill.
The bark is taken off.
The logs are cut into little chips.
The chips are cooked in huge vats
of water until they turn to mush.

The mush goes onto a huge screen.
Giant rollers press the mush flat.
The water is squeezed out.

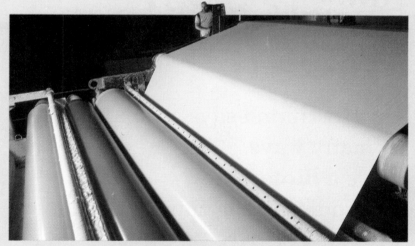

Soon the mush dries into long sheets.
The sheets are rolled into one
huge roll of paper.

Think About It
What do you use paper for?

How do animals talk to each other?

Ms. Clark's Class
Edwards Elementary School
Las Vegas, Nevada

Dr. Herrnkind says animals talk
in many ways.
He is a **biologist**.
He studies living things.

Sometimes animals talk
to each other with sounds.
Crickets chirp, frogs croak, and
wolves howl.
Often, they make the sounds to tell
other animals where to find them.

Dr. Herrnkind says touch is a way
of talking, too.
A cat licks her kittens so that they
know she is their mother.

Sometimes animals change their looks.
Some birds spread bright feathers
to show they are looking for a mate.

Animals even use odors to talk.
A skunk says to stay away
with its odor.

William Herrnkind

Unit Two
Physical Science

Physical science is about how
things work.
It is learning how machines work.
It is learning what makes things
move.
It is learning how sounds are made.

Lesson 8
Comparing

Getting Started

Making a Bar Graph

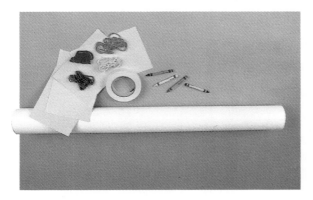

1. Use large paper, yarn, tape, crayons, and drawing paper.

2. Work with partners. Mark how tall each partner is.

3. Tape a yarn end at each mark. Let the other end reach the floor.

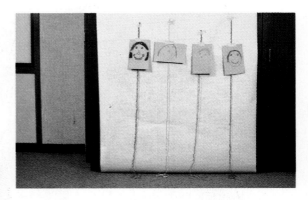

4. Tape a picture of yourself to your yarn. Look at all the yarns. See how tall they are.

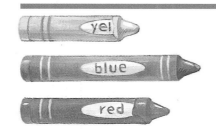

The boy is **comparing** belts.
He places the belts side by side.
The yellow belt is longer.
The purple belt is shorter.

The buildings are tall.
Which building is tallest?

The red brush is wider than
the green brush.
The blue brush is the widest.

The blue rug has more squares.
It has more **area**.
The pink rug has fewer squares.
It has less area.

Things take up **space**.

Look at the boxes in the picture.
The girl doll is bigger.
It takes up more space in the box.
The boy doll is smaller.
It takes up less space.

The big elephant is heavier.
It **weighs** more.
The small elephant is lighter.
It weighs less.

A **balance** can show which
thing weighs more.

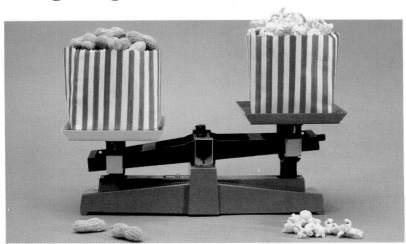

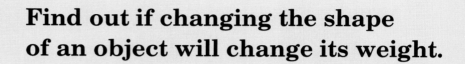

Finding Out

Use these things:
clay
balance

Find out if changing the shape of an object will change its weight.

1. Make two balls of clay.
Place them on the balance.
Make the balls weigh the same.

2. Make a snake with each clay ball.
Make one snake longer than
the other.
Weigh the snakes.

3. Make a pancake with each
clay ball.
Make one thinner than the other.
Which pancake do you think
will weigh more?
Weigh the pancakes and find out.
Were you correct?

**Did the shape change
the weight of the clay balls?**

Lesson 8 Checkup

1. Look at each group of objects.
Tell how the objects compare.

2. Which car takes up less space?

3. Think! Tell how you could
compare these ribbons.

Lesson 9
Measuring

Getting Started

Making a Measuring Tape

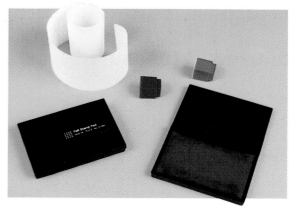

1. Use a strip of paper, a pencil, two blocks, and two ink pads.

2. Use the blocks to make prints. The picture shows you how.

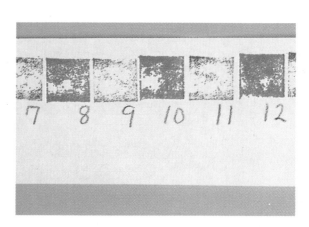

3. Number the prints.

4. Use the strip to measure things.

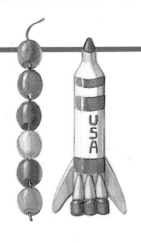

We **measure** to find the size
of something.
We can measure with different things.

Crayons are used to measure
the toy boat.
The boat is 3 crayons long.
Each crayon is one **unit**.

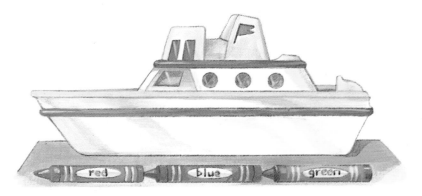

The unit in this picture is a paper clip.
How long is the boat, now?

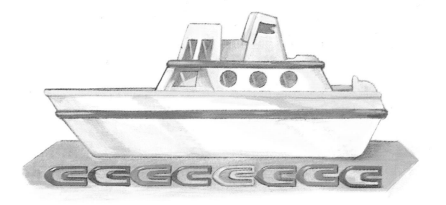

People need units that are
the same size all over the world.
One of these units is the **meter**.

The boys are measuring the tree.
They are using meter sticks.
A meter stick is 1 meter long.
The tree is about 2 meters tall.

Another unit is also the same size everywhere.
This unit is the **centimeter**.
We measure things with
a centimeter ruler.
The centimeter ruler has
centimeter units marked on it.

The caterpillar is 8 centimeters long.

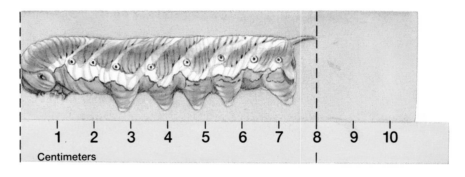

How long is the leaf?

Sometimes it is easier to use
a meter unit to measure an object.
Sometimes it is easier to use
a centimeter unit.
Look at the pictures.
Which unit would you use
to measure each object?

Finding Out

Use these things:
chart
tape
centimeter ruler

Find out if you can estimate how long some objects are.

1. Get a small object.
Tape it to the chart.

2. Estimate how long the object is.
Write your estimate on the chart.

3. Measure the object.
Write the measurement on the chart.

4. Tape other objects to the chart.
Keep estimating and measuring.
Write your estimates and
measurements on the chart.

Did your estimates get better?

Lesson 9 Checkup

1. Tell how long the feather is.

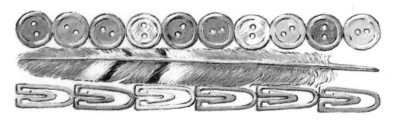

2. Use a centimeter ruler.
Tell how long the feather is.

3. Tell if you would use centimeters
or meters to measure each object.

4. Think! Use a centimeter ruler.
Which ant will get to the food first?

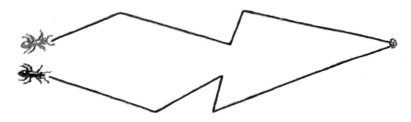

Lesson 10
Making Things Move

Getting Started

Moving a Ball

1. Use a table tennis ball and some blocks.
Work with partners.

2. Set the blocks on a table.
Make a maze.

3. Put the ball on the table.
Work together.
Blow the ball through the maze.
Do not let it go off the table.

Things move all around you.
Pushes and pulls make them move.

The wind pushes and the kite moves.
The horse pulls and the sled moves.

Pushes and pulls are called **forces**.
Where do you see forces in the picture?

A force can change the way
something moves.

The girl pulls.
The pull makes the dog go slower.

The woman pushes.
The push makes the swing go
another way.

This basket is heavy.
It takes a big force to make
the basket move.

This basket is light.
A small force can make it move.

This path is rough.
It takes a big force to make
the wagon move.

This sidewalk is smooth.
A small force can make
the wagon move.

 # Finding Out

Use these things:
string
paper clip
rubber band
2 books
centimeter ruler

Find out if pulling a heavier object takes more force.

1. Work with a partner.
Tie the string around one book.
Bend a paper clip.
Hook the paper clip to the string
and to the rubber band.

2. Put your finger into the rubber band.
Pull the book over your desk.
Watch the rubber band stretch.
Have your partner measure
how long the rubber band is.

3. Put a second book on top
of the first book.
Pull both books with the rubber band.
Have your partner measure how long
the rubber band is now.

Which time was more force needed?

Lesson 10 Checkup

1. Which takes more force?
Why?

or

or

2. Think! Tell where each box will move.

Lesson 11
Machines

Getting Started

Making a Model Wagon

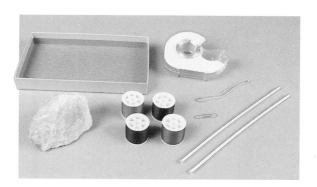

1. Use a box, tape, straws, spools, a paper clip, a rubber band, and a rock.

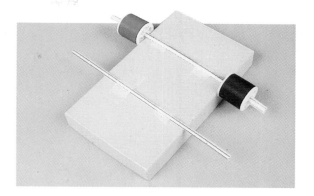

2. Tape straws to the box. Put spools on the straws. Put tape around each straw next to the spool.

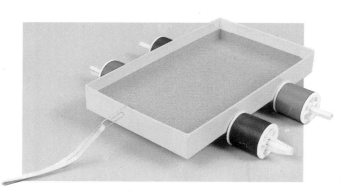

3. Tape a bent paper clip to the box. Loop a rubber band through the paper clip.

4. Pull the rock slowly across your desk. Put the rock inside the box and pull again.

We use **machines** every day.
They can make work easier.
Some machines have many parts.

Some machines have only a few parts.

A **wheel** is a machine.
A wheel makes it easier to move things.

A **lever** is a machine, too.
A lever makes it easier to move things.

A **ramp** is another machine.
A ramp makes it easier to move
things up.

Finding Out

Use these things:
ruler
crayon
clay

Find out how a lever works.

1. Put a crayon under the ruler.
Place a ball of clay on one end
of the ruler.

2. Push down at the other end
of the ruler to lift the clay.
Feel the force needed.

3. Move the crayon closer to the clay.
Push down again.
Feel the force needed now.

Which way needed less force?

Lesson 11 Checkup

1. Which of these are machines?

2. Match the words with the pictures.

lever   wheel   ramp

 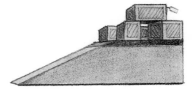

3. Think! Draw a picture to show
how you could use each thing
to make work easier.

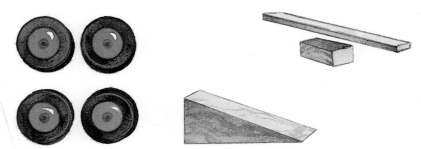

Lesson 12
Making Sounds

Getting Started

Making Sounds with a Ruler

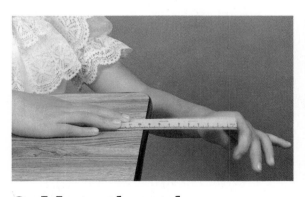

1. Use a ruler.
Put it on your desk.
Let one end
stick over the edge.

2. Hold one end.
Snap the other end.
Watch the ruler.
Listen to the sound.

3. Move the ruler.
Make less stick out.
Snap the ruler.
Listen to the sound.

4. Move the ruler again.
Make even less stick out.
Snap the ruler again.
Listen to the sound.

Sounds are made when things move.

The strings in the pictures move
back and forth very fast.
They **vibrate**.
The vibrations make sounds.

Sometimes you can see things vibrate when sounds are made.
Sometimes you can feel them vibrate.
But most times you cannot see or feel things vibrate.

Things in the pictures are vibrating. Which things could you see or feel when they vibrate?

Sounds can be loud or soft.

Blowing into a horn makes the air inside vibrate.
Blowing harder makes the air vibrate more.
The sound is louder.

Blowing softly makes the air vibrate less.
The sound is softer.

Sounds can be high or low.

Small things vibrate faster.
They make higher sounds.

Big things vibrate slower.
They make lower sounds.

Which bell in the picture makes
a higher sound?
Which makes a lower sound?

Sounds are all around you.
They are made by many things.

Machines make sounds.
Water and wind make sounds.

You make sounds.
You talk, sing, and shout.
You use **vocal cords** in your throat.
The vocal cords vibrate.
You make sounds with other
body parts, too.

Animals make sounds.
Some animals use vocal cords.
Some animals use other body parts.

 **Finding Out**

Use these things:
soda straw
scissors

Find out what sounds a straw can make.

1. Press one end of a straw flat.
   ◇ **Sharp!** Cut a V at the flat end.

2. Put the V end in your mouth.
   Press down with your lips.
   Blow into the straw.
   Listen to the sound.
   Feel the vibrations.

3. Keep blowing.
   ◇ **Be Careful!** Cut off
   a small piece of the straw.
   Listen to the sound.

4. Keep blowing.
   Keep cutting off small pieces.
   Listen to the new sounds.

How does the sound change?

Lesson 12 Checkup

1. Look at each picture.
   Tell what vibrates to make a sound.

2. **Think!** How could you use
   this object to make a soft sound?
   To make a loud sound?
   To make a low sound?
   To make a high sound?
   How could you make
   the sound stop?

Lesson 13
Sounds Move

Getting Started

Using a String Telephone

1. Use paper cups,
paper clips, string,
and a sharp pencil.

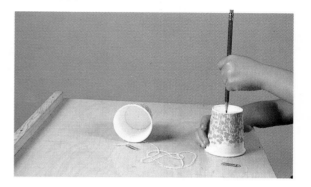

2. Poke a hole in each cup.
Put string through
the holes.
Tie each end
to a paper clip.

3. You and a partner
each take a cup.
Stretch the string tight.

4. Talk softly into one cup.
Ask your partner
to listen.

A gong makes sounds when it is hit.
The gong vibrates.
This makes the air around it vibrate.
You cannot see these vibrations.
The vibrations move out from the gong.
They move out in all directions.

Soon the vibrations get to your ear.
Things in your ear vibrate.
Then you hear the sounds.

Sounds move through the air.
They move through other things, too.
They move through things like
wood and glass.
And they move through water.

Sounds bounce off things that are smooth and hard.
They bounce off things the way a ball bounces off a wall.
Sounds that bounce off things are called **echoes**.

The room in the picture is empty.
The walls and floor are smooth and hard.
Sounds from the girl make echoes.
The room is noisy.

Sounds are soaked up by soft things.
They are soaked up like a ball
that is thrown into a pillow.

The room in the picture has soft
curtains and a rug.
They soak up sounds.
The room is quieter than an empty
room.

What things can you name
that soak up sounds?

Finding Out

Use these things:
2 self-lock bags
pencil

Find out how well sounds move through different things.

1. Blow into one bag.
   Fill it with air and close it tightly.
   Put the bag on a desk.

2. Fill the other bag with water.
   Close it tightly.
   Put the bag on the desk.

3. Put your ear on the desk.
   Tap the desk with a pencil.
   Listen to how loud the sound is.

4. Put your ear on the air bag.
   Tap the desk and listen to the sound.

5. Put your ear on the water bag.
   Tap the desk and listen to the sound.

Which time was the sound softest?

Which time was the sound loudest?

Lesson 13 Checkup

1. The bird is making sounds.
How do the sounds get to the girl?

2. What do the sounds move
through in this picture?

3. Think! Suppose that sounds
could not move through air.
How would your classroom
be different?

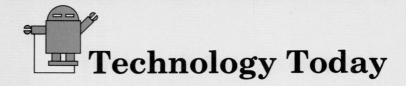 # Technology Today

Robots Help Us

Robots help us in many ways.
Some are toys to play with.
Many do work in factories.
Some robots do work in space.
Others do work in the ocean.
One kind of robot even teaches
tricks to animals.
Someday, robots may do work
in your home.

A robot is a machine.
It has a computer for a brain.
But it cannot think.
People must program the computer.
The computer tells the robot
what to do.

Think About It

Pretend you have a robot.
What will you have it do?

Why can we hear some sounds and not others?

Ms. Dean's Class
Cahill Elementary School
Edina, Minnesota

You can hear many sounds.
But some sounds are too high
or too low for you to hear.

Dr. Henoch is an **audiologist**.
She studies hearing.
Dr. Henoch says your ears were
made to hear only some sounds.
They are sounds that help keep
you safe from danger.

You can hear thunder and sirens.
Hearing them helps keep you safe.
But you do not need to hear very
high or very low sounds to keep safe.

Some people cannot hear sounds
that other people can hear.
They have hearing problems.
Sometimes hearing aids or other
things will help them hear better.
Dr. Henoch helps people with
hearing problems.

Miriam Henoch

Unit Three
Earth Science

Earth science is about
the ground and sky.
It is about rocks and soil.
It is about the sun and stars.
It is about seasons.
It is learning why these things
are important to you.

Lesson 14
Rocks

Getting Started

Grouping Rocks

1. Use rocks, a hand lens, a crayon, paper, and a tray.

2. Look closely at each rock. Feel each rock.

3. Find rocks that are alike. They can be alike in size, color, how they feel, or in other ways.

4. Group all the rocks. Label each group. Tell how the rocks are alike.

Rocks can be one color or many colors.
They can be shiny or dull.
Rocks can be rough or smooth.
They can be rounded or jagged.
Most rocks are hard.
Some rocks are not very hard.
They break apart easily.

Rocks are always changing.
They change very, very slowly.
Water and wind change rocks.
They wear away rocks.
Larger rocks get smaller.
And smaller rocks get even smaller.

Rocks are everywhere.
They are on top of the ground.
They are deep under the ground.
And they are on the bottoms
of oceans and streams.

People long ago used rocks
for many things.

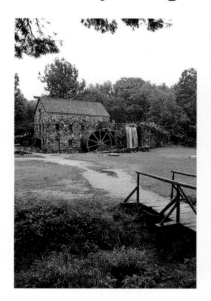  

People today use rocks
in many ways.
What ways can you name?

Finding Out

Use these things:
5 small, jagged rocks
plastic jar with lid
can
white cloth
rubber band
hand lens

Find out how rocks can change.

1. Cover the top of a can with cloth.

2. Put five rocks in a jar.
Cover the rocks with water.
Put the lid on the jar tightly.

3. Shake the jar hard for 5 minutes.
What do you think will happen
to the rocks?

4. Take the lid off and slowly pour
the water into the can through
the cloth.
Take out the five rocks.
Look closely at the cloth
with a hand lens.

What did you see in the cloth?

Where did they come from?

Lesson 14 Checkup

1. Name three places you can find rocks.

2. How do water and wind change rocks?

3. Look at each pair of rocks.
   Name some ways the rocks are alike.
   Name some ways they are different.

A   B

4. **Think!** What ways could you use these rocks?
   Name as many ways as you can.

Lesson 15
Soil

Getting Started

Looking at Soil

1. Use soil, a hand lens, a tray, a crayon, and drawing paper.

2. Spread the soil around on the tray.
Feel the soil.
Smell the soil.

3. Look at the soil.
See what different parts you can find.

4. Draw circles on the paper.
Put a different part of soil in each circle.

Soil covers the ground in many place
It is made of tiny pieces of rock and
pieces of living things that have died

Soil can have many things in it.
It can have air and water in it.
Soil can have plants and animals
that are alive in it.

Soil has many spaces in it.
Air and water fill the spaces.
Dry soil has air in most of the spaces.
Wet soil has water in most
of the spaces.

Plants and animals in the soil get air
and water from the spaces.

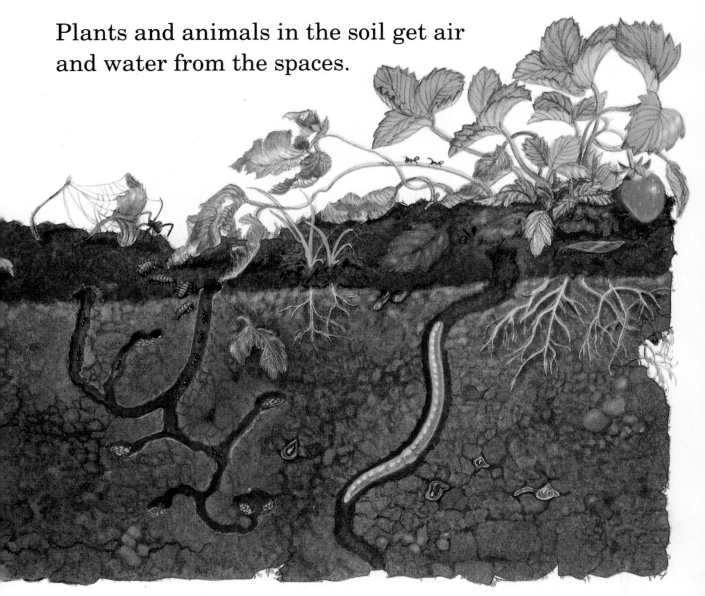

There are many kinds of soil.
Most soil is red, brown, or black.
Some soil is loose and grainy.
Some soil is soft.
Other soil is hard and rocky.

Living things need soil.
Many animals use soil for homes.
Most plants grow in soil.

People need soil, too.
We use plants that grow in soil.
We use them for food and clothing.

Finding Out

Use these things:
2 jars
2 kinds of soil
measuring cup

Find out how much air is in soil.

1. Label one jar *soil A*.
Put one kind of soil in the jar.
Fill it halfway.

2. Label the other jar *soil B*.
Put the other soil in this jar.
Fill it halfway.

3. Pour the same amount of water
into each jar.
Watch the air bubbles come up.

4. Compare the bubbles in each jar.

Where did the air come from?

Where did the water go?

**Did both soils have the same
amount of air in them?**

Lesson 15 Checkup

1. Which things make up soil?

2. Which things are found in soil?

3. Where do animals that live in soil get air and water?

4. Think! What would happen if all the soil were suddenly gone.

Lesson 16
The Seasons

Getting Started

Making a Seasons Circle

1. Use a paper plate, old magazines, paste, crayons, and scissors.

2. Draw lines across the paper plate. Print the name of a season in each part.

3. Cut out pictures that show seasons. Paste them onto the plate where they belong.

There are four parts to a year.
Each part is a **season**.
The four seasons are spring, summer,
fall, and winter.

In spring, the days begin to get longer.
It is warmer and often rainy.
Then spring turns to summer.
The days get even longer.
It is hot in many places.
There is less rain.

Summer turns to fall.
The days get shorter.
It is cooler and often windy.
Then fall turns to winter.
The days are shortest in the winter.
It is cold and snowy in many places.
In time, winter will turn to spring.
The days will once again get longer.

The seasons keep changing.
How does what you do change
with the seasons?

Spring is the time for new life.
Many animals have babies.
New plants grow.
Old plants get new leaves and flowers.
Birds come back from warmer places.
Many animals wake up from their
winter rest.

Summer is the time to grow.
Animals have lots of food to eat.
Baby animals grow bigger and
stronger.
Plants grow bigger, too.
They grow more stems and leaves.
Many plants grow flowers and fruit.

Fall is the time animals and plants
get ready for winter.
Some animals store food.
Some animals get warmer coats.
Many birds fly to warmer places.
The leaves of some plants change
color and fall to the ground.

Winter is the time to rest until spring.
There is less food for animals to eat.
Some animals eat food they
have stored.
Other animals do not eat at all.
Some plants rest.
Other plants die.

Finding Out

Use these things:
large paper
paints
paintbrushes
tape
newspapers

Find out and show what seasons are like where you live.

1. Choose a season.
   Think about what the season is like where you live.
   Think about how hot or cold it is.
   Think about what people wear.
   Think about what plants and animals do.
   Ask a grownup if you do not know.

2. Paint a picture of the season.
   Show if it is sunny or rainy.
   Show people, plants, and animals.

3. Help the class put all the season paintings in order.
   Tell about your painting.

What are seasons like where you live?

Lesson 16 Checkup

1. Which season am I?

I have the longest days. ____?____

I have the shortest days. ____?____

I am cool and often windy. ____?____

I am warm and often rainy. ____?____

2. The pictures show something about each season.
Put the seasons in order.

3. Think! How will the picture have changed when winter comes?

Lesson 17
The Sun and Stars

 **Getting Started**

Comparing Sizes Near and Far

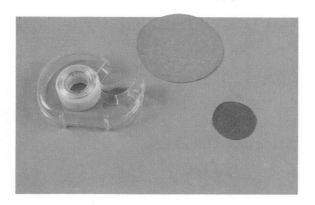

1. Use tape, a small circle, and a big circle that will be put on a wall.

2. Hold the small circle the way it is held in the picture.

3. Walk backward until the circles seem to be the same size.

4. Walk backward some more until the big circle looks smaller. Why does it look smaller?

Look up at the sky on a clear night.
You can see many **stars**.
Stars are like huge balls of fire.
But they look like tiny dots of light
because they are so very far away.

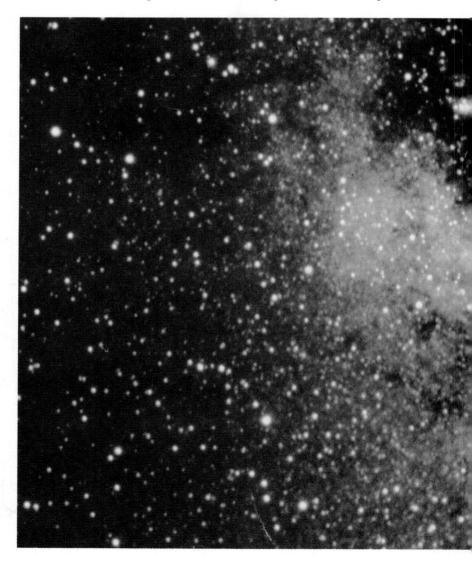

Some stars make pictures in the sky.
A group of stars that makes a picture
is called a **constellation**.
The Big Bear is a constellation.
Can you find the Big Dipper
in the constellation?

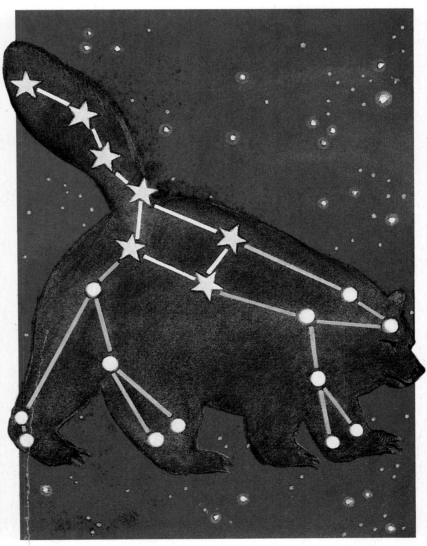

The **sun** is a star.
It is the only star we see in daytime.
It looks larger than other stars
because it is so much closer to us.

The sun is very bright and very hot.
It gives us **light** and **heat**.

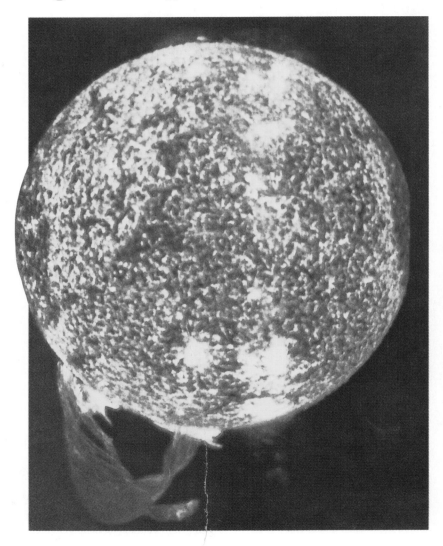

Light from the sun is important
to living things.
Animals and people must have
light to see.

Plants use light from the sun to grow.

Heat is also important to living things.
Sunlight warms the ground and water.
Heat from the ground and water
warms the air.
The heat from the ground, water, and
air helps keep living things warm.

Sometimes people use sunlight
to heat water for homes.

Some places get a lot of sunlight.
The sunlight makes the air hot.
Other places get less sunlight.
The air is cooler.

You can measure how hot the air is.
You can use a **thermometer**.
The numbers tell you the temperature.

🔍 Finding Out

Use these things:
2 glasses
2 thermometers
drawing paper

Find out if sunlight heats water.

1. Put some cold water in the glasses.
Put the same amount in each.
Label one glass *sun*.
Label the other glass *no sun*.
Place a thermometer in each glass.

2. Make a chart for temperature.
Read the thermometers.
Write the numbers in the chart.

3. Put the *sun* glass in a sunny place.
Put the *no sun* glass in a shady place.

4. Wait for two hours.
Read each thermometer again.
Write the numbers in the chart.

Which glass had warmer water?

Does sunlight heat water?

Lesson 17 Checkup

1. Fill in the blanks with these words.

thermometer   sun   heat   Big Bear   star

The sun gives us light and ___?___.

The sun is a ___?___.

Our closest star is the ___?___.

One constellation is the ___?___.

We measure temperature with a ___?___.

2. Tell why each thing needs the sun.

3. Think! What would the sun look like from a star?

Technology Today

From Rocks to Jewelry

Some rocks are special because
they are pretty and very hard.
These rocks are called **gems**.
We often use gems in jewelry.

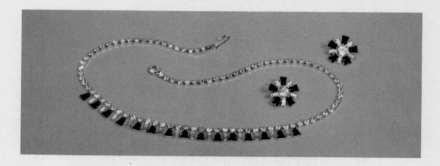

Gems are hard to find.
They may look dull in the ground.
They may be hidden in other rocks.

Most gems become pretty only
when they are cut and polished.
A grinding wheel cuts smaller and
smaller pieces off the gem.
Soon the gem is the right shape.
Then a polishing wheel makes it smooth.

Some gems are cut to look rounded.
Others are cut so that they have
many flat sides called faces.

Think About It

How would you use a gem?

Ask a Scientist

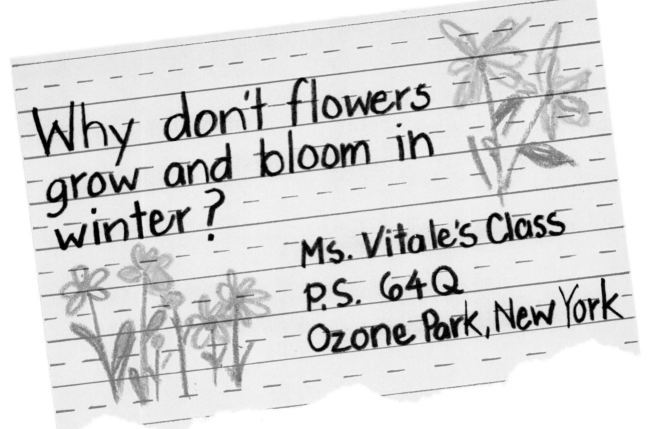

Why don't flowers grow and bloom in winter?

Ms. Vitale's Class
P.S. 64Q
Ozone Park, New York

Dr. Mullin is a **botanist**.
A botanist is a scientist who studies plants.

Dr. Mullin says that days get shorter in the fall.
Nights get longer.
These things make changes happen inside plants.

Many plants lose their leaves
in the fall.
They cannot make food without
leaves.
And they cannot grow and bloom
without food.

Days get longer in the spring.
Nights get shorter.
New changes happen inside plants.
Many plants grow new leaves
in the spring.
They begin to make food again.
Then many plants bloom, too.

Beth Mullin

Unit Four
Health Science

Health science is about you
and your body.
It is learning how you show
what you feel.
It is learning how your senses
help you find out about things.

Lesson 18
You Are Special

🔍 Getting Started

Making a Picture of You

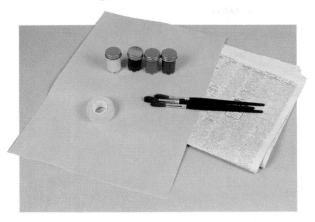

1. Use drawing paper, newspapers, paints, a paintbrush, and tape.

2. Paint a picture of you. Show how you look.

3. Tape your picture on a wall. Tell about how you look. Tell about things you like to do.

People are alike in many ways.
They are also different in many ways.
People can be short or tall.
They can have different colors
of hair, eyes, and skin.
Each person is special because
each person is different.
How are you special?

You are special because no one else looks or thinks quite the way you do. You are also special because you have different **feelings** at different times. When have you felt happy or sad? When have you felt angry or afraid?

You show your feelings in your
own way.

Some ways to show your feelings
are better than others.
How do you show that you are
happy or sad?
How do you show that you are
angry or afraid?

Other people have feelings, too.
Sometimes they feel sad or afraid
just as you do.
Kindness can help them feel better.

How is this boy showing kindness?

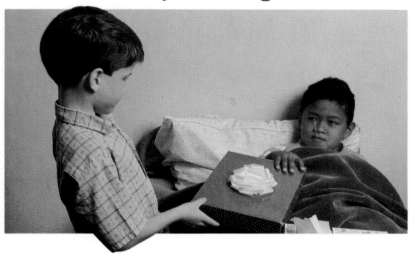

How can these children show kindness?
Name some ways you show kindness.

Finding Out

Use these things:
mirror
drawing paper
crayons

Find out how your face can show feelings.

1. Look at your face in a mirror.
   Make happy faces.
   Draw a picture of something that makes you happy.

2. Look in the mirror again.
   This time make sad faces.
   Draw what makes you sad.

3. Make angry faces.
   Draw something that makes you angry.

4. Make your face show that you are afraid.
   Draw a picture of something that makes you afraid.

Did your face show different feelings?

1. Match the word to the picture.

  happy
sad

 angry
sad

  afraid
happy

 sad
angry

2. Name some ways that you are special.

3. Think! Tell a story about the picture.
Tell what you could do to show kindness.

Lesson 19
Seeing and Hearing

Getting Started

Using Your Eyes and Ears

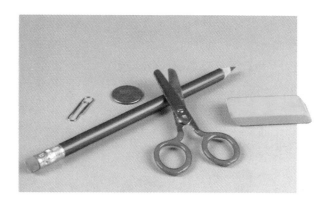

1. Use a paper clip,
a coin, a pencil,
an eraser, and scissors.

2. Look at the objects.
Tell about each one.

3. Close your eyes.

4. Have your partner
drop one of the objects.
Name the object that
was dropped.

You use your **senses** every day.
They help you learn about things
around you.

Seeing is one of your senses.
You see with your eyes.

You can see colors and sizes.

How are the birds alike?
How are they different?

You can see shapes with your eyes.
Look at the picture.
What different shapes do you see?

Where does each piece belong?
How do you know?

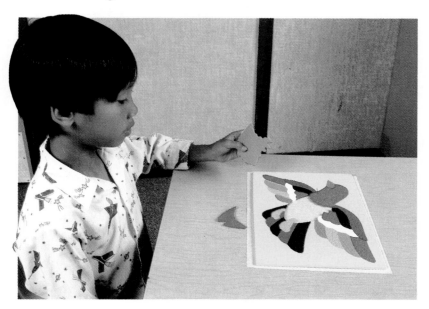

Hearing is another sense.
You hear sounds with your ears.
Hearing helps you learn
about things.

Things in the pictures are making
sounds.
What sounds would you hear?

You must take care of your ears and eyes.
Keep your ears safe from loud sounds.
Keep things out of your ears and eyes.
Have your ears and eyes checked.

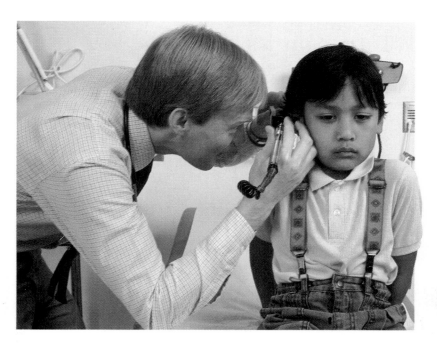

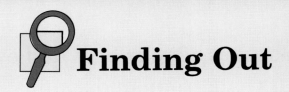

Finding Out

Use these things:
coins
crayons
pencils
triangles
squares

Find out how color, shape, and size help you tell about objects.

1. Work with a partner.
   Get objects from your teacher.

2. Put the objects on your desk.

3. Think about one of the objects.
   Tell your partner about the object.
   Do not name it.
   Tell about its color.
   Tell about its shape and size.

4. Ask your partner to name
   the object.

**What words did you use to tell
about each object?**

Lesson 19 Checkup

1. What do you use to learn about each thing?   eyes   ears

2. Tell how to keep your ears safe from loud sounds.

3. Think! These pictures are from objects around you.
Tell what you think each object is.

Lesson 20
Smelling and Tasting

Getting Started

Smelling Things

1. Use signs and things to smell.

2. Look carefully at this picture. Smell things as the picture shows.

3. Smell each thing.

4. Put each thing with the right sign.

Smelling is one of your senses.
You use your nose to smell **odors**.
Smelling helps you learn about things.

Things in the picture have odors.
What would the odors tell you?

Things in these pictures have odors.
What would the odors tell you?

You must take care of your nose.
You should smell things in a safe way.

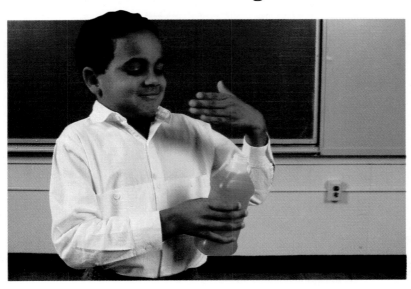

sweet

sour

salty

Tasting is another sense.
You use your tongue to taste things.
You can learn about things
when you taste them.
You can learn if things are sweet.
You can learn if things are sour.
And you can learn if things are salty.

Look at the big picture
at the top of the page.
How would each thing
in the picture taste?

Be careful when you taste.
Use your eyes and nose before you taste.
Never taste or smell some things.

⌕ Finding Out

Use these things:
pieces of raw apple
pieces of raw pear
blindfold
paper plate

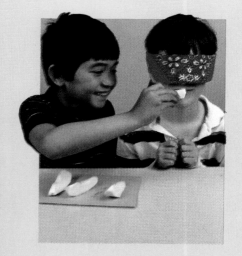

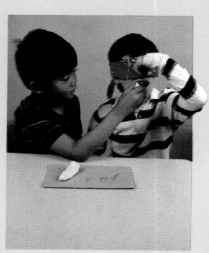

Find out which senses work together.

1. Wash your hands.

2. Work with a partner.
Get two pieces of apple and
two pieces of pear.

3. Put on a blindfold.

4. Have your partner give you
one of the foods.
Then have your partner give you
the other food.

5. Now hold your nose.
Have your partner give you
one of the foods and then
the other food.
Can you tell what you tasted?

Which two senses work together?

✓ Lesson 20 Checkup

1. What do you use to learn about
each thing?   tongue   nose

2. These things make odors.
Which odors will tell about danger?

3. Think! Why can't you taste
food well when you have a cold?

Lesson 21
Touching

Getting Started

Touching Objects

1. Use a box of objects that your teacher gives you.

2. Do not look in the box. Shake the box.

3. Find two objects that are alike.

4. Put the two objects together.

Touching is one of your senses.
You use your skin to touch things.

You can touch with your hands
and feet.
You can touch with all of your skin.

Touching helps you learn about things.

You learn if things are rough or smooth.

You learn if things are hard or soft.

Touching helps you learn
if something is hot or cold.
Touching helps you learn
if something is wet or dry.

You must take care of your skin.
Cover your skin to keep it safe
from very hot and very cold things.

Use your eyes before you touch
things.

Too much sun can hurt your skin.
What can you do to keep your skin
safe from too much sun?

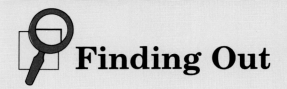

Finding Out

Use these things:
orange
peach
apple
tennis ball
mittens
tray
blindfold

Find out what can change your sense of touch.

1. Work with a partner.
   Put some things on a tray.

2. Look at the things for 10 seconds.

3. Put on a blindfold.
   Have your partner mix up
   the objects.
   Feel each thing.
   Tell your partner what you touch.

4. Put on the mittens.
   Have your partner mix up
   the objects again.
   Touch each thing.
   Tell your partner what you touch.

How did the mittens change your sense of touch?

Lesson 21 Checkup

1. Choose the word that matches the picture.

hard   wet

soft   dry

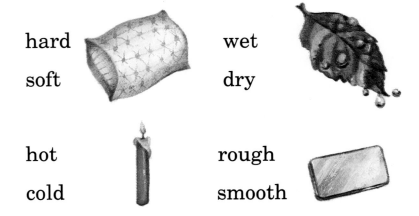

hot   rough

cold   smooth

2. How can you safely carry a very hot bowl of soup?

3. **Think!** Say four words that tell how this thing would feel.

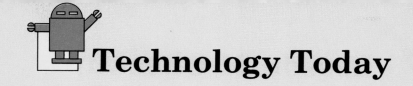

Technology Today

Seeing More with Microscopes

A **microscope** is an important tool in science.
It makes small objects look bigger than they really are.

One kind of microscope is the light microscope.
It has two special pieces of glass called lenses.
One lens gathers light from an object.
The two lenses together make the object look bigger.

light microscope

snowflake

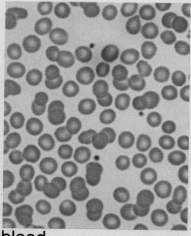

blood

Another kind of microscope
is called an electron microscope.
It can make objects look even bigger.
These pictures were taken with
an electron microscope.

house dust

black fly

aphids

Think About It

Why do you think it is important
to make things look bigger?

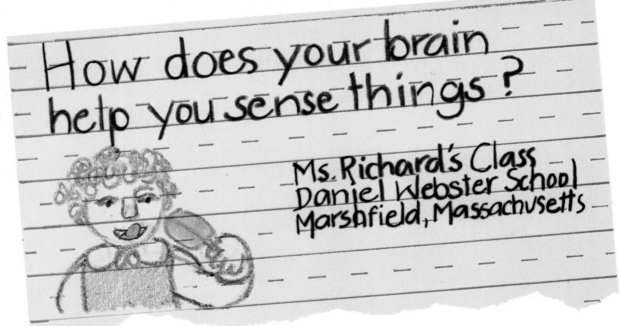

How does your brain help you sense things?

Ms. Richard's Class
Daniel Webster School
Marshfield, Massachusetts

Dr. Harper is a **professor**.
He teaches college students
who want to be doctors.

Dr. Harper says your brain
does not sense things all by
itself.
It gets messages from your
eyes, ears, nose, tongue, and skin.
The messages move along nerves
inside your body.
Nerves are like tiny wires.

Your eyes see shapes and colors.
They send messages to your brain.
Then your brain tells you what
the shapes and colors mean.
Your eyes may see a stop sign.
Then your brain tells you to stop.

Your ears may hear your name.
Then your brain tells you to listen.

Edwin Harper

Glossary

A

animal page 16
A living thing that moves from place to place and finds its own food. *Elephants, butterflies, turtles, and robins are animals.*

area page 81
The flat space that something covers. *The blue rug has more area than the pink rug.*

audiologist page 130
A person who studies hearing. *The audiologist checked my hearing.*

B

balance page 83
A tool that shows which thing is heavier. *You can use a balance to find out if an orange is heavier than a lemon.*

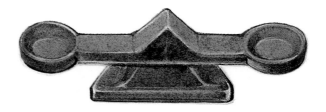

biologist page 74
A person who studies living things. *The biologist watched the birds use twigs to make a nest.*

body covering page 32
The outside part of an animal.
*Feathers, fur, scales, and shells
are body coverings.*

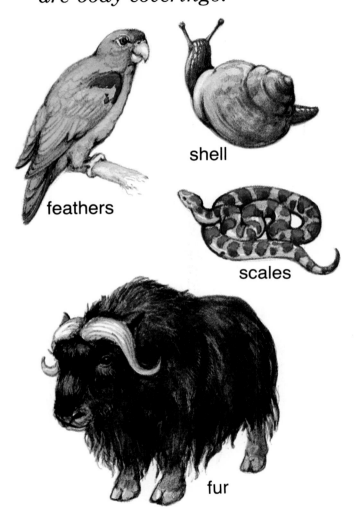

feathers

shell

scales

fur

botanist page 172
A person who studies plants.
*The botanist watched the
bean seed grow into a plant.*

C

centimeter page 90
A small unit for measuring
how long or wide something
is. *My little finger is
1 centimeter wide. I measured
it with a centimeter ruler.*

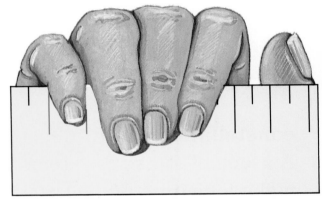

compare page 80
To find out how things are
alike and different. *He is
comparing the three crayons
to see which one is longest.*

cone page 53
The part of some kinds of trees that has seeds inside. *A brown cone fell from the pine tree.*

constellation page 163
A group of stars that seems to make a picture. *My favorite constellation is the Big Bear.*

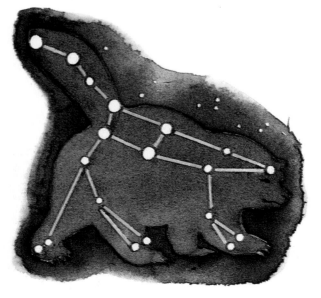

E

echo page 124
A sound that you hear over again. *You can hear echoes when you yell inside an empty room.*

F

feeling page 179
Happy, sad, angry, or afraid. *I had a happy feeling when my grandma hugged me.*

flower page 53
The part of a plant that is often colorful and makes seeds. *He picked a red flower from the rose bush.*

force page 96
A push or a pull. *Forces can make things move.*

The boy is pushing.

The boy is pulling.

fruit page 53
The part of a plant that holds the seeds. *Apples and pears are fruits.*

G

gem page 170
A special kind of rock that is pretty and very hard. *Gems can be used for jewelry.*

H

hearing page 188
One of your five senses that uses your ears. *Hearing helps you learn how things sound.*

heat page 164
Warm or hot. *The heat from sunlight keeps us warm.*

K

kindness page 181
A friendly or nice way of acting. *I showed kindness to my sad friend by talking to her.*

L

leaf page 52
The flat, thin part of a plant that grows on the stem. *The leaves of that tree give our yard shade.*

lever page 107
A tool used to make it easier to move things. *She used the board as a lever to lift up the rock.*

light page 164
Something that you must have to see. *You use light from the sun to see.*

M

machine page 104
A tool that makes our work easier. *Wheels, levers, and ramps are machines.*

measure page 88
What you do to find the size of something. *I like to measure myself to see how tall I am.*

meat eater page 24
An animal that eats other animals. *A fox is a meat eater.*

meter page 89
A large unit for measuring how long or wide something is. *The door is 1 meter wide. I measured it with a meter stick.*

microscope page 208
A tool that makes tiny things look larger. *You can see tiny parts of a hair with a microscope.*

move page 18
To go from one place to another. *Animals move by walking, flying, swimming, or crawling.*

O

odor page 194
A smell. *The rotting garbage had a bad odor.*

P

paper mill page 72
A factory where paper is made. *Wood chips are cooked, dried, and made into paper in a paper mill.*

plant page 48
A living thing that makes its own food and does not move from place to place. *Trees and grass are plants.*

plant eater page 24
An animal that eats plants. *A rabbit is a plant eater.*

professor page 210
A person who teaches college students. *The professor explained to the students how eyes help people see.*

R

ramp page 107
A tool that makes it easier to move things up or down. *He pushed a box up the ramp.*

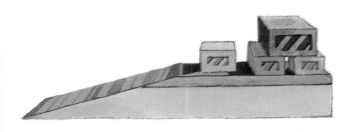

robot page 128
A machine that does some things a person can do. *Some robots can teach tricks to seals for animal shows.*

rock page 136
A hard thing that can be found in and on the ground everywhere. It has never been alive. *I used rocks to make a strong wall.*

root page 50
The part of a plant that grows down into the soil. *A carrot plant has one large root.*

S

season page 152
One of the four parts of the year. *The seasons are spring, summer, fall, and winter.*

seed page 53
The part of a plant that can grow into a new plant. *Fruits have seeds inside.*

seeing page 186
One of your five senses that uses your eyes. *Seeing helps you learn how things look.*

senses page 186
Ways your body helps you learn about the world. *The five senses are seeing, hearing, smelling, tasting, and touching.*

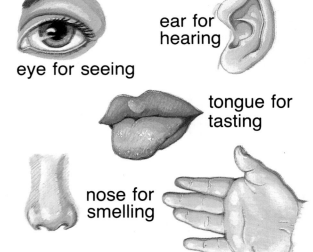

eye for seeing

ear for hearing

tongue for tasting

nose for smelling

skin for touching

smelling page 194
One of the five senses that uses your nose. *Smelling helps you learn how things smell.*

soil page 144
Dirt. *The roots of plants grow in soil.*

sound page 112
What you hear when something vibrates. *Music, honking, and talking are sounds.*

space page 82
An open place for things to fit into. *A big car takes up more space than a small car.*

star page 162
One of the dots of light you see in the sky at night. *Stars are like huge balls of fire and are very far away.*

stem page 51
The part of a plant that holds the leaves and flowers. *The stem of a plant can be hard or soft.*

stem

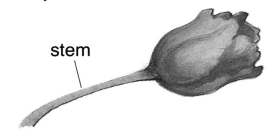

sun page 164
The bright star you see in the sky during the day. *You get light and heat from the sun.*

T

tasting page 196
One of the five senses that uses the tongue. *Tasting helps you learn if things are sweet, sour, or salty.*

temperature page 68
How hot or cold something is. *The temperature of the soup is hot.*

thermometer page 167
A tool that measures how hot or cold a thing is. *You can use a thermometer to measure how hot the air is.*

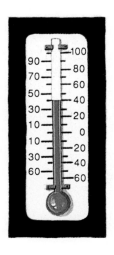

touching page 202
One of the five senses that uses the skin. *Touching helps you learn if things are rough or smooth, hard or soft, hot or cold, wet or dry.*

U

unit page 88
One of something. *We used a block as a unit to measure how tall the vase is.*

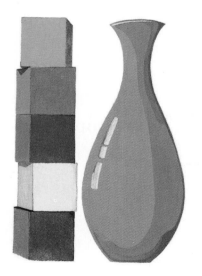

V

vibrate page 112
To move back and forth very fast. *Things make sounds when they vibrate.*

vocal cords page 117
The part of the throat that vibrates when you make talking sounds. *You use your vocal cords when you sing.*

W

weigh page 83
To be heavy or light. *A heavy book weighs more than a light feather.*

wheel page 106
A round tool that makes moving things easier by rolling. *A wagon moves easily because it has wheels.*

wild page 66
Living things that do not live with people. *Wild bears live in the forest and take care of themselves.*

Acknowledgements

Illustration Acknowledgements

Kitty Diamantis p. 80, 88A-C
Marlene Howarton p. 112, 122A, 213BC, 217A, 218BC, 219C, 220C, 221AB, 222AB
Kirchoff/Wohlberg
  K/W/Susan Lexa p. 212C, 215AD, 216A
Lois Lovejoy p. 152, 212AB, 213A, 214ABC, 215BC, 216B, 217B, 218AD, 219AB, 220ABD, 222C
Debbie Morse p. 124, 125, 167BD
Sharron O'Neil p. 90, 144-45, 154-55, 156-57
Mel Peterson & Associates
  MP&A/Will Giles p. 58
  MP&A/Sandra Pond p. 50BC
  MP&A/Michael Woods p. 16, 24, 26AC, 32, 40, 42AB, 66
Pronk & Associates
  P&A/Alan Barnard p. 122
  P&A/Barbara Massey p. 68, 136, 144A, 162, 178, 186, 188, 194, 196, 202
  P&A/Steve Pilcher p. 48, 49
  P&A/Paul Rivoche p. 187
Publishers' Graphics Inc.
  PG/Helen Davies p. 29, 55, 109, 191
  PG/Marie DeJohn p. 37, 63, 85, 93, 119, 149, 169, 199
  PG/Pam Johnson p. 21, 45, 71, 101, 127, 183, 207
  PG/Steven Schindler p. 159
D.J. Simison p. 81, 96, 104

Photo Acknowledgements

4B Bill Ross/West Light; 4CB Spencer Swanger/Tom Stack & Associates; 4CT Bill Ross/West Light; 4T A. Blank/Bruce Coleman Inc.; 6 Lynn M. Stone/Animals, Animals; 7B Stacy Pick/Stock, Boston; 7T Cary Wolinsky/Stock, Boston; 12 A. Blank/Bruce Coleman Inc.

Lesson 1: 14 M. Philip Kahl; 16BL Stephen Dalton/Animals, Animals; 16BR Stephen J. Krasemann/DRK Photo; 16CL Ron Goor/Bruce Coleman Inc.; 16CR Jen & Des Bartlett/Bruce Coleman Inc.; 16T Peter Ward/Bruce Coleman, Inc.; 17BL E.R. Degginger/Animals, Animals; 17BR Zig Leszczynski/Animals, Animals; 17CR Patrice Ceisel/Stock, Boston; 17TL C. Allan Morgan/Peter Arnold, Inc.; 17TR Patrice Ceisel/Stock, Boston; 18BL John R. MacGregor/Peter Arnold, Inc.; 18BR Zig Leszczynski/Animals, Animals; 18C Tom Brakefield; 18T M.P. Kahl/Bruce Coleman Inc.; 19BL Ed Cesar/National Audubon Society/Photo Researchers; 19BR Perry D. Slocum/Animals, Animals; 19T E.R. Degginger/Animals, Animals; 21L Ted Levin/Animals, Animals; 21R Souricat/Animals, Animals

Lesson 2: 22 John Gerlach/Click-Chicago; 24L Millard H. Sharp/Click-Chicago; 24R Grant Heilman Photography; 24T Leonard Lee Rue III/Animals, Animals; 25B Runk-Schoenberger/Grant Heilman; 25T John Cancalosi/Tom Stack & Associates; 26B R.S. Virdee/Grant Heilman; 26T Tom Brakefield/Bruce Coleman Inc.; 27BL Wardene Weisser/Berg & Associates; 27BR Miriam Austerman/Animals, Animals; 27TL Ralph A. Reinhold/Animals, Animals; 27TR R.H. Armstrong/Animals, Animals

Lesson 3: 30 James P. Rowan; 32BL David M. Dennis/Tom Stack & Associates; 32 BR Runk-Schoenberger/Grant Heilman; 32 T Richard P. Smith/Tom Stack & Associates; 33B Zig Leszczynski/Animals, Animals; 33 CL Wardene Weisser/Berg & Associates; 33CR C.B. Frith/Bruce Coleman Inc.; 33TL Gunter Ziesler/Peter Arnold, Inc.; 33TR Larry Lipsky/Tom Stack & Associates; 34B S.L. Craig, Jr./Bruce Coleman Inc.; 34TL Steve Kaufman/Wildlife Photobank; 34TR Carlye Calvin; 35BL Leonard Lee Rue III/Tom Stack & Associates; 35BR Zig Leszczynski/Animals, Animals; 35TL Joe McDonald/Bruce Coleman Inc.; 35TR Patti Murray/Animals, Animals

Lesson 4: 38 Jonathan T. Wright/Bruce Coleman Inc.; 40B Robert P. Carr/Bruce Coleman Inc.; 40T Grant Heilman Photography; 41T Grant Heilman; 43BL Stephen Frink/The WaterHouse, Inc.; 43BR Stephen Frisch*; 43TL J.C. Carton/Bruce Coleman Inc.; 43TR Brent Jones

Lesson 5: 46 Jim Brandenburg/DRK Photo; 48L Tom Stack/Tom Stack & Associates; 48RB Grant Heilman Photography; 48RC John Shaw/Tom Stack & Associates; 48RT Breck P. Kent/Earth Scenes; 49BL Hans Reinhard/Bruce Coleman Inc.; 49BR Neville Fox-Davies/Bruce Coleman Inc.; 49TL Jim Yuskavitch/Tom Stack & Associates; 49TR Kevin Byron/Bruce Coleman Inc.; 51L E.R. Degginger/Earth Scenes; 51RT Donald Specker/Earth Scenes; 53BC Grant Heilman Photography; 53BL Neville Fox-Davies/Bruce Coleman Inc.; 53TC E.R. Degginger/Earth Scenes; 53TR Robert P. Carr/Bruce Coleman Inc.

Lesson 6: 56 Steven C. Kaufman/Peter Arnold, Inc.; 59BL Frank Siteman/Stock, Boston; 60R Thomas Kitchin/Tom Stack & Associates; 61BL Jeffrey Muir Hamilton/Stock, Boston; 61TL Dick George/Tom Stack & Associates; 61TR Mike Mazzaschi/Stock, Boston

Lesson 7: 66BL David M. Doody/Tom Stack & Associates; 66BR Robert P. Carr/Bruce Coleman Inc.; 66T Phil Degginger/Click-Chicago; 68B Jeff S. Share; 68T Phil Degginger/Bruce Coleman Inc.; 69T Grant Heilman Photography; 72L Thomas Kitchin/Tom Stack & Associates; 72R Donald Dietz/Stock, Boston; 73B John Blaustein/Woodfin Camp & Associates; 73T Weyerhaeuser Company; 75B Florida State University; 75T K.W. Fink/Bruce Coleman Inc.; 76 Bill-Ross/West Light

Lesson 8: 80B Chris Bensley/Stock, Boston; 83T Peter Davey/Bruce Coleman Inc.; 91BL Jen and Des Bartlett/Bruce Coleman Inc.; 91BR © David Schaefer; 91CR Jane Burton/Bruce Coleman Inc.; 91TL G.I. Bernard/Earth Scenes

Lesson 10: 94 Brian Parker/Tom Stack & Associates; 96T Michael Kevin Daly/The Stock Market

Lesson 11: 102 Holt Studios Ltd/Earth Scenes; 104B John Shaw/Tom Stack & Associates; 104CL Breck P. Kent/Earth Scenes; 104CR Bob McKeever/Tom Stack & Associates; 104TL Christopher Morrow/Stock, Boston; 104TR Tom Campbell/West Light; 105C Stephen Frisch*; 106B Tim Davis; 106T Chuck O'Rear/West Light; 107B Chris Brown/Stock, Boston; 107TL Elliott Varner Smith*

Lesson 12: 113B Michael Kevin Daly/The Stock Market; 113TR Carlye Calvin; 116BL Tom Braise/The Stock Market; 116BR Stuart Cohen/Stock, Boston; 116T Spencer Swanger/Tom Stack & Associates; 117BL Henry Ausloos/Animals, Animals; 117BR Hans Reinhard/Bruce Coleman Inc.; 117T Mark Reinstein/Click-Chicago

Lesson 13: 120 Chris Sorensen/The Stock Market; 123B Brian Parker/Tom Stack & Associates; 123TL F. Stuart Westmorland/Tom Stack & Associates; 128L Dr. E.R. Degginger; 128R Dick Durrance II/Woodfin Camp & Associates; 129 Tom Sobolik/Black Star; 131B Rick Browne*; 131T Arjen Verkaik/The Stock Market; 132 Spencer Swanger/Tom Stack & Associates

Lesson 14: 134 Stewart M. Green/Tom Stack & Associates; 137 Dale Jorgenson/Tom Stack & Associates; 138B Pictor/DPI; 138TL George Schneegass; 138TR Mark E. Gibson/The Stock Market; 139BR D.P. Hershkowitz/Bruce Coleman Inc.; 139TC V.A. Satterwaite/The Stock Market; 139TL John Colombaris/The Stock Market; 139TR Jeff Foott/Tom Stack & Associates

Lesson 15: 142 Frank Morgan/DPI; 146BL James P. Rowan/Click-Chicago; 146BR Don L. Crawford/Click-Chicago; 146TL Fred Myers/Click-Chicago; 146TR Jon Feingersh/Tom Stack & Associates; 147B J. Howard/Stock, Boston; 147TL Raymond G. Barnes/Click-Chicago; 147TR John Gerlack/Animals, Animals

Lesson 16: 150 © Len Rue Jr.; 152B Phil Degginger/Click-Chicago; 152T Harry Hartman/Bruce Coleman Inc.; 153B Dr. E.R. Degginger; 153T Bruce Barthel/The Stock Market

Lesson 17: 160 William Edward Smith/The Stock Market; 162 U.S. Naval Observatory; 164 NASA; 165B Black Mamba/DPI; 165TL Mark Gibson/The Stock Market; 165TR S.D. Halperin/Earth Scenes; 166B Jay Nadelson/The Stock Market; 166TL Peter Menzel/Stock, Boston; 166TR Souricat/Animals, Animals; 167B G.L. Kooyman/Animals, Animals; 167T Gary Milburn/Tom Stack & Associates; 170B Dr. E.R. Degginger; 171B Benn Mitchell/The Image Bank; 171T Fred Ward/Black Star; 173B Dr. Beth Mullin; 173T Rod Planck/Tom Stack & Associates; 174 Bill Ross/West Light

Lesson 18: 176 Michael Chan/The Stock Market; 178B Norma Morrison; 178TR L.L.T. Rhodes/Click-Chicago; 179BR Richard Kolar/Animals, Animals; 179TL Jon Feingersh/Tom Stack & Associates; 180B Peter Fronk/Click-Chicago; 180TL Gay Bumgarner/Click-Chicago; 180TR Lawrence Manning/Click-Chicago

Lesson 19: 186A Barth Schorre/Bruce Coleman Inc.; 186B John H. Hoffman/Bruce Coleman Inc.; 186C Michael Habicht/Animals, Animals; 186D Wayne Lankinen/Bruce Coleman Inc.; 186E W. Perry Conway/Tom Stack & Associates; 186F Barth Schorre/Bruce Cole-man Inc.; 186G Laura Riley/Bruce Coleman Inc.; 188B Michael Fogden/Animals, Animals; 188T Richard Pasley/Stock, Boston

Lesson 20: 195TR Clyde H. Smith/Peter Arnold, Inc.

Lesson 21: 202B Clare Brett-Smith/Bruce Coleman Inc.; 204BR Thomas Hovland/Grant Heilman; 205TL Grant Heilman/Grant Heilman Photography; 208C L. West/Bruce Coleman Inc.; 208L Dr. E.R. Degginger; 208R Dr. E.R. Degginger; 209B David Scharf/Peter Arnold, Inc.; 209TL David Scharf/Peter Arnold, Inc.; 209TR David Scharf/Peter Arnold, Inc.; 211B IUPUI Publications/Rick Baughn

Wayland Lee*/Addison-Wesley Publishing Company: 40 insets, 41B, 41 inset, 51B, 52, 53BR, 53TL, 58, 59BR, 59T, 60L, 61 insets, 81, 83B, 91TR, 105B, 106CL, 136, 141, 170T, 191, 196 insets, 196T, 197BR, 203, 205TR, 207, 211T

All other photographs taken expressly for the publisher by Tim Davis.

Front cover: Gary Milburn/Tom Stack & Associates
Back cover: Joe McDonald/Tom Stack & Associates

*Photographs taken expressly for the publisher

Special thanks to: Escondido School, Stanford, CA; Juana Briones School, Palo Alto, CA; Laneview School, San Jose, CA; Ponderosa School, Sunnyvale, CA; Pomeroy School, Santa Clara, CA; Selby Lane School, Redwood City, CA; Willow Oaks School, Menlo Park, CA; Renee Lynn; Maya Clifton; Cindy Cohen; Clark Dunbar; Anne Fitzpatrick; George Fry; Joanne Hendricks; Shirley Kraus; Mike Masiello; Susie Robbins; Sandra Stahl; Sherry Sykes; Bomber; Happy Hollow Zoo, San Jose, CA; Great America, Santa Clara, CA; Palo Alto Extended Day Care, Palo Alto, CA; Santa Clara 4-H, Santa Clara, CA; YMCA Sequoia, Redwood City, CA; and Ted & Lindsey Merendino.